Write it! Publish it! Sell it!

Sell it!
The complete guide to marketing, promoting and selling your book

Adam Jackson

Contents

Preface

From the author of Write it! How to write your book in 30 hours or less, and Publish it! How to self-publish your book for free using KDP, CreateSpace and Smashwords comes this complete guide to marketing, promoting and selling your book.

If you have a published book, whether self-published or traditionally published, or you are currently writing a book then this guide is for you.

You will discover a wide range of methods you can use to propel your book up the bestseller lists and generate the income you desire. You will be able to plan your marketing strategy using the methods you prefer or those that have the potential to get the best results.

Sell it! is that next step towards increasing your sales and developing a fan base. It's never too soon to start marketing your book - plan and action your strategy today.

Introduction

Marketing and sales are part of the writing business, if you want to see your book sales rise and make a good income from your writing you need to actively engage with this aspect of your business. Even if you are a traditionally published writer you can expect your publisher to ask for your marketing strategy – yes your publisher may undertake some promotional activity however there will be an expectation that you will plan and undertake activities that will generate and maintain interest in you and your book.

If the thought of marketing scares you a little – fear not. There are so many opportunities available for you to engage with your readers that you may find you enjoy this aspect of your business as much as the actual writing. You can promote your book through face to face activities, social media, or by creating promotional materials such as videos.

You can promote your book effectively even if you have a zero budget. Whilst some of the methods and ideas included in this book have both free and paid for options, you can decide if and when you allocate a budget to marketing and where it is best spent.

If you have, or are looking to secure, a traditional publishing contract you will find that some of the tasks in this book are completed by the publisher, however don't ignore them as they can be useful when pitching your book to an agent or publisher; for example understanding where your book will sit on the bookshelf (categories), knowing which published books are similar to yours, and demonstrating a commitment to marketing, which is now expected by all publishers, can only help you and your book move off the slush pile and receive a second reading.

Throughout this book your potential readers and customers will be referred to as your readers – they just might not know it yet. Ensure your readers see your book and tell them why this is a book they should read, it's then only a short step to the checkout.

When marketing your book you need to consider your readers' behaviour in order to identify where to concentrate your efforts during the lifetime of your book. When a reader looks for a book in a traditional bookstore they look at any offers, locate the section that interests them, scan the shelves (focusing on the shelves that are within their eye line), note covers, titles and authors, pick up any books that appeal, read the blurb, read any reviews, they may read the first page, note the price and then buy or discard. When readers browse online the process is the same, offers, categories, titles, covers and authors (first page of search results is the eye line), click on books that appeal, read the description, read the reviews, browse inside if available, check the price and then buy or discard. Get your title, cover and other key aspects of your book right and it will quickly move from the shelf to the reader's basket.

Once your reader has read your book they will want more from you; they will seek you out online, listen out for that radio interview and attend your next book launch – they will have become a loyal fan, make sure you look after them.

The first chapters of Sell it! cover how to make your book visible to your readers; this includes creating a title, cover and description that reinforces the message "*this is a book for you.*" They also include selecting categories and keywords, and getting reviews. Later chapters cover different methods to engage, and develop and maintain a relationship with your readers both online and offline; these methods can then be used to develop your marketing strategy.

Read this book through and then create a marketing plan that is right for you, your book and your readers; review this plan at regular intervals and add new ways to engage with your readers.

Start planning your marketing strategy today; even if you haven't written a single word you can start generating interest and building anticipation for that launch. You may even find you have a massive following of readers all ready to hit that *Buy Now* button as soon as your book is published.

1 - Title

You've written a great book, one that you want readers to enjoy. Now is the time to create a great title – your book deserves it. Your readers will scan the titles and covers of the books they can see; your title needs to grab their attention and then hold it. If the title attracts the reader they will start on the journey to making a purchase, reading those pages and becoming a fan of your work. Your readers need to feel that this book is exactly what they are looking for – maybe because it answers their questions, maybe because it makes them laugh, maybe because they see themselves in the title. Whether fiction or non-fiction the title makes a promise to the reader that they will be entertained and informed. The title will say "*this is a book for someone like you*," and possibly "*this book will change your life*."

Titles are also used by search engines to propel your book onto the first page of search results so it is vital to consider what words and phrases your readers might use and enter into search engines when looking for the genre or topic of your book, or indeed similar topics where your book could meet their needs. If your main title is not search engine friendly, often the case with fiction as your book is unlikely to be titled *a thriller set in the eighteenth century*, consider using a sub-title; this does not have to appear on your cover. Sub-titles enable you to provide further information about your book and tend to be more descriptive than main titles, for example *a concise history of 20th Century Spain*, or *a political thriller set in modern day Egypt.*

Never underestimate the importance of your title or sub-title being search engine friendly; the majority of all purchases start on the internet even if your reader eventually buys from the high street; if your reader does not see your book they will not buy it.

If you have a traditional book publishing contract your title may be changed by the publisher. Even if this is the case it is still important to go through the process of creating an appealing title because, prior to offering you a contract, your agent or publisher will note your title and this needs to create a positive first impression; your publisher may even decide that your title is in fact perfect for your book. If your title is changed you can use the results of creating a title – a collection of words and phrases – with other promotional material and activities.

Ensure you allow adequate time for this task; if you have spent a year or more writing your book then spending a week getting the title right has got to be a good investment. Consider what your book is about and write down all the words and phrases that come to mind. Perhaps you have some great phrases in your book – seek them out and write them down. Look at the titles of other successful books in your genre, look at the titles of other successful books in any genre. Write down the locations and characters in your book, the subject matter and any interesting facts. All of these words and phrases can help you build or inspire the perfect title.

Complete the tasks below to generate words, phrases and title ideas. Write them all down. As you make notes you may come up with additional title ideas, write these down as well.

• Write down any titles you already have in mind, even if they are only half formed.

• Write a description or list of words and phrases related to the content of your book, this could include characters, location, theme, topic, problem, or solution. As you do this titles may spring to mind for example the name of a character (Lucy), a location (The Turret), an event (The Crash), or a solution (The Ideal Career).

• Use search engines to find words and phrases readers are entering when searching online. Using both a search engine (Google) and an online bookstore's search feature (Amazon) type in words related to your book. First note what search phrases are suggested, these are likely to be the most searched for terms, next note the words and phrases that appear in your search results. Write down any that appeal and any potential titles.

• Using an online book retailer look in the categories where your book might appear – write down titles, subtitles, and phrases from book descriptions that appeal to you; take particular note of the bestsellers.

• List the benefits to the reader of the content of your book, for example, follow these suggestions and you can live clutter free, increase your income, or become a better manager.

• List how a reader might feel or think whilst reading your book – transported to a time when spending your whole life in servitude was the norm for many girls. Your novel may challenge readers' beliefs, if this is the case write this down – this will challenge the way you think about the homeless.

• Have a look at titles you like, maybe books you have purchased yourself, could you change one or two words so that you create something that has familiarity however is different. This can also have the effect of causing the reader to spend a little longer looking at your title to ensure they are reading it correctly, as long as this is a positive experience and they don't feel deceived then they will take the next step towards making that purchase.

• Use a book or website of proverbs, sayings, clichés, metaphors or similes; these can be a really useful sources of titles – a stitch in time, a bird in the hand, the calm before the storm. Change these slightly or combine elements to create something new. For example first impressions could become final impressions, and absence makes the heart grow fonder could become the absent heart.

• Use mind-mapping or word association to generate even more words that relate to your book.

• The most useful source of title ideas is your book. Read through carefully and highlight any words or phrases that could grab the attention of a reader, you'll be surprised at what you find in your own writing. You may have written "each year he painted the gate, each year he painted it green. This was probably the only constant in his life." From this you might think of the title - the green gate. If you have written a book on dieting or eating disorders you may have written "the food just seemed to call out, as if it was talking to me, telling me to consume more and more." You might come up with title - the language of food.

Once you have all of your words, phrases and title ideas you can start to construct your perfect title. Generally, though not always, a main title will be short whilst the sub-title will be longer and more descriptive – remember this is a guideline and you can create what works best for your book. You can work on the title and sub-title separately or you may choose to work on them together.

Below are a number of different approaches you can take. Experiment with each of them as, even if you don't want to use that particular approach, the title you come up with may inspire something new. Some of these approaches may appear to be better suited to non-fiction however don't discount them – some excellent fiction titles include words like *how to* or *guide to*. You may choose to combine different approaches – perhaps a question as the main title and a how to for the sub-title:

• Ask a question – Do you want to lose 10lb in 2 weeks? How far is it to the moon? Questions can be very effective in non-fiction as they elicit a response from the reader – hopefully one that will lead them to buy the book. Questions also work in fiction as they can set the tone and create a feeling.

• Make a promise – Follow this plan and you will lose 10lb in 2 weeks.

• Create a guide or how to - How to fly a kite. A guide to Rome in a day. This could be extended to include a target market – A guide to Rome for families.

• Speak directly to your target market – Exercise for the over sixties. Over thirty and single.

• Answer the concerns of your reader – Lose 10lb in 2 weeks without giving up any foods you enjoy.

- Provide solutions – Rid your life of clutter forever.

- Use numbers – 10 ways to…. 40 days in….

- Use a name of a character, location or event – The Mountain.

- Use a characteristic, job role, or physical feature – Hook, Hunchback.

At this stage you will have a list of possible titles. Use different coloured highlighter pens to categorise your titles into yes, no and maybe. Concentrate on those you have highlighted as yes; whittle these down to your top five. Consider if and how you can improve them – use a dictionary or thesaurus to ensure you have used exactly the right words. Ask friends or other writers to give you feedback, you could even hold a vote on your Facebook page.

Finally select the best title for your book.

2 - Cover

Your readers will judge your book by its cover; no matter how good the content is they will never make it to page one if the cover does not attract and appeal. A great cover will grab the reader's attention; when they see it they will pick up your book or click on the image and want to read the description.

Your cover needs to make a promise to the reader, it needs to say *"this is a book for someone like you," "this book is like other books you have enjoyed,"* or *"this book will provide you with the solution you've been looking for."* Think about what your book has to offer the reader – will it make them laugh, excite, inform, entertain, is it thought provoking, a tragedy, is it set in the future, the past or present? Will it give your reader a glimpse of a life they aspire to, or maybe it provides a solution that will help them achieve their goal.

If you have a traditional publishing contract your publisher may take on sole responsibility for creating the cover with no input from you. If you use a self-publishing service that includes cover design you may or may not be able to input into this process. If you self-publish you will have sole responsibility for the cover, you can of course outsource this task however you will still need to provide a brief and approve the design.

If you are creating the cover yourself then follow the guidance below – if you are outsourcing your cover you still might find the exercise useful in order to get a feel for what you want and to provide a brief:

• Take some time now to write a list of words or short phrases that describe the essence of your book; you may find it useful to write this as a blurb or sales pitch and then highlight those words and phrases that jump out at you. You can use the list you created for your title however add to this to include words that are closer to the feeling of, or how you want your readers to feel about, your book – professional, fun, humorous, rich, travel, vintage, modern, tragic, dark, money.

• Read through your book again - do any scenes particularly stand out? Make a note of or highlight them.

• Look at other covers in your genre or subject – note any common characteristics, anything that appeals and also things you don't like; pay particular attention to the bestsellers.

When you have your list select three to five words or phrases and use them to inspire your cover design. Alternatively select and make notes about a scene from your book that you would like to recreate as a cover. Add any specific design or style features you might want to add. Your list might look like this:

- Funny
- 3 young ladies (they don't know each other and never meet)
- 1 man (he knows each of the ladies)
- Vintage feel.

Or

- Scene where Joanna is stood in the rain looking back at her home just before she leaves this house for good
- Needs to have an air of sadness but also anticipation
- Set in the early sixties.

Or

- Money saving tips
- Busy person
- Shopping
- Popular look, not too serious.

Once you have these phrases you can start to sketch out your cover - for an ebook you only need a front cover, for a printed book you will need a full cover. Spend some time going back to your list and generating visual interpretations of what you want your cover to say and how you want your reader to feel. You don't need drawing skills, simple stick people, box houses and a few notes are sufficient.

Note: your cover does not have to include images – you could use blocks of colour and text; this is simple, effective and achievable. Many classics use this format.

Front cover
The reader will usually see the front cover first either on screen or when they take the book from a shelf. This is your shop window so use it well. You can include photos, drawings, text, in fact anything that can be displayed visually. As you design and create your cover ensure you have enough space for any text (usually the title and author name), that this text can be easily read and that is does not hide important aspects of the cover image. If the cover is for a printed book do not have any important parts of the image or text near the edges as this may be cut during the printing and binding process. Darker edges are

preferred to ensure your book stands out against the white background of online retail sites.

Back cover

It is best to keep the back cover simple and uncluttered because you need some space for your description or blurb and other details relating to your book such as bar code and price. This could be a continuation of the landscape or background from your front cover – again look at examples for ideas. If you find your description does not stand out or is difficult to read then consider placing a single block of colour onto the back cover to contain your text.

Spine

The spine can be a continuation of the front and back cover or you could use a separate strip of colour. Depending on the depth of your spine you could also include text – typically this is the title, series name and/or author. Make a note of the depth of the spine, if you are going to create a wrap-around cover ensure you add this to your total cover measurements.

Text

When you have your cover outlined it is time to think about the position, size and type of text. Decide what text you want or need on the front, back and spine – this might include title, author, series name, publisher, blurb, barcode and price. Make notes about where each will appear or write it onto your sketch, also make notes about colour, size and font type.

Options for creating your cover
Once you have an outline of your cover you can start to create or outsource it. You have a number of options including:

Online tools and templates – many online self-publishing services, including KDP and CreateSpace, offer online cover creation tools with templates and photos. You can create a professional looking cover quickly, easily and for free. You can even add your own photos, drawings and text. Check terms and conditions as you may find that if you use the supplied templates and photos you will not be able to use that cover should you decide to publish your book using other services; this is not a problem it just means your book may have multiple covers. This is probably the easiest way to get started with cover design and creation.

Purchase a self-publishing package – many self-publishing packages offer cover design alongside a range of other services including proofreading, editing, printing, storage and distribution. How much input you have into the design process will depend on the package you select and the terms you negotiate. There are some excellent companies who offer tailored packages to meet your needs however there are still some vanity publishers around so ensure you seek recommendations and look at samples of work. Check the ownership and usage rights of covers created using these services as you may need to create a new cover should you choose to publish elsewhere.

Hire a professional – whether you use an agency, a recommended individual or someone on Fiverr.com remember that a well-designed cover sells books. Whilst this option has a cost - ranging from £/$5 - £/$1000s - you do not need a huge budget; there are a number of online sites where professionals offer their services for a fixed or negotiable price. You can get a cover designed on Fiverr.com for just $5; whilst the price is low the quality can be high, many excellent designers choose to offer their services in order to build a client base and get reviews or just to earn some additional income doing something they love. At these prices you could commission three or four cover designs and select the best.

Do it yourself – you can create your cover yourself using hand drawing or painting techniques, or computer software. If using computer software you don't need to be highly skilled in this area, keep things simple and you can produce a good cover that will attract readers.

When you create your cover there are a few things to note: use a limited palette (your computer software may offer you a selection), ensure your cover works well when displayed in greyscale (some ereaders), ensure your cover works when reduced in size (online retailers), have edges that will show up against a white background, and note the required size and resolution for your selected publication method and service.

Depending on your skillset you can either draw or paint your cover and then scan it onto your computer or you can use photo editing or image creation software. If you do not have suitable software give Gimp a try, this is available for free and includes a useful range of tools.

Save your image in a suitable format for your chosen publication methods, usually jpeg or pdf, and always save a master copy in the image editing software format so you can easily make changes later - you can make changes to a jpeg or pdf however some features such as layers may not be preserved.

Using photographs

A simple way to create a great looking cover is to use one or more photographs and apply a transformation to them. The filters and effects available to you in photo editing software makes it possible to create something unique. You could take a single photo and change the lighting and colour balance, or convert it to greyscale. You could take a collection of photographs and create a montage, or cut various elements from each – landscape, animals, people, cars, or trees – and put them together to make a new scene or arrangement.

Once you have your completed image you could transform it further – how about converting it into a cartoon effect, pen and wash, or watercolour; this can also be a great way of illustrating children's books.

You can take your own photos or purchase them online from sites such as iStockphoto.com. When purchasing photos check the usage rights, they may be royalty free however you may have a maximum number of uses or you may not be able to transform them.

Different covers for different markets
Whilst initially you will probably create one cover for your book; at a later date you might decide to create different versions to appeal to different markets. You could have an adult cover, a teenage cover and a film version cover. You can also have different covers for your ebook, printed book and audio book.

Making changes
If you have self-published your book you can change your cover at any time; for some writers changing their cover has resulted in a significant increase in sales. You could start by creating a cover using an online cover creator and later, when budget allows, commission a new one.

Whichever route you take ensure that your cover not only stands its ground amongst other books on the shelf but also stands out from the crowd.

3 - Description

The description for your book has the potential to clinch that sale. You've hooked them with your title, captivated them with your cover and now you can sell your book with a description that reinforces the message that this is a book the reader must have and must read. The description expands on the promise of the title and cover; after reading it your reader will want your book and want it now.

The description will appear on your sales page of online book retailers and on the back cover of your book, sometimes the version on the back cover is a shorter blurb. It will also be used by search engines to bring your book to the attention of readers; as you know if they don't see it they won't buy it.

Find out how many characters or words you have available for your description and make best use of them. If you write ten words and truly believe this is all that needs to be said and the readers will "get it" or be hooked and want more then use ten words, however, more words are usually better. This is a time when your writing should be at its best, if the description does not engage the reader, or worse disengages them, they will decide the book is not for them.

If you have a traditional publishing contract you will get support for this activity; you may even find the task done for you. If you self-publish you will need to do this yourself or outsource it. This is one area of marketing where you already have the skills to do a great job – you are a writer after all – although you may need to use slightly different techniques as you want your reader to say "*I must have this book now,*" and be in no doubt that they are going to read this book.

Whether fiction or non-fiction the basic principles are the same, your description should:
- Provide information about the book
- State the benefits to the reader
- Describe how the reader will feel
- Identify any unique content or features
- Address the reader directly
- State any similarities to other books and authors
- Be search engine friendly.

You will already have a selection of words, phrases and descriptive text generated whilst creating your title and cover, if you skipped these chapters go back and complete the tasks, use these to put together a compelling description ensuring you have included the most commonly searched for words and phrases related to your book. Use descriptive paragraphs, lists, questions, benefits, or a mixture of these.

Examples
The selection below are paragraphs that could be included as part of a description.

• Marie closed the door for the last time intending never to return to her old life. Little did she realise that three years later that life would come back to haunt her.

• Twenty nutritious meals that can be made using supermarket ingredients, prepared in just 20 minutes, and stored for use during the week.

• A thriller that will have you on the edge of your seat, if you enjoy reading (another author) you will love this book.

• If you lead a busy life, have a full-time job, and find you just never have enough time to plan, prepare and cook nutritious meals for yourself and your family then this book is for you.

Note: avoid pricing information in the description as your retailer may change the price, your book might be available in different currencies and VAT changes may affect the price.

Whatever you write and however you pitch your book ensure your writing shines. Check for spelling errors, particularly for those commonly misspelt words. Ask readers or authors to give feedback on your description. This is an important piece of marketing material – make it work hard.

4 - Categories and Keywords

Most publishing and sales platforms ask you to select which category or categories you want your book to appear in; they also provide you with the opportunity to add a number of keywords or phrases. Use these features to best advantage and your readers will find your book quickly and easily.

Categories

Putting your book into a category that is right for its subject or genre maximises the chance of it being seen and bought. However the right category is not necessarily the most obvious category. Many retail sites include promotional features such as *other books in this category* and *customers also bought*, so selecting the right category can pay dividends.

If you select a popular category with 1000s of books you might find yours is initially displayed on page 124 meaning your readers may never see it; when was the last time you clicked through to page 124?

If you select a small category with only a few hundred books it may be easier to get your book displayed on page 1 or 2 however, check out the sales rankings (number of books sold), if readers rarely buy from this category then this is not going to help your sales either.

Take some time searching an online bookstore and looking at the available categories and sub-categories. Note which categories books similar to yours appear in, also note categories your book could fit into. For each of these categories get a feel for how many books are available. Look at the top ten bestsellers and ascertain, through sales or bestseller ranking, how many copies are being purchased.

Ideally you want to place your book in a category that has few titles and high sales – lots of readers and little competition – and is also a good fit for your book, in reality you will need to select categories that are as close to this as possible.

Once you have completed your research rank the categories you have identified as suitable for your book in order of preference based on best fit, number of books, and sales. Depending on where you publish you may be able to select more than one category; if this is the case enter them in order of preference.

When you enter the categories at the publication or listing stage you may find that the choices you have available are not an exact match for the categories on the retail site, don't worry, just choose the best match.

If you have written, or are writing, a series it is perfectly OK to place your books into different categories, you can then monitor which provide the best returns.

This is an area you can experiment with, if you find that your book is not getting a high ranking in your chosen categories, or you are not making many sales, then change the category.

Keywords and phrases
Online publishers and retailers will provide you with the opportunity to list a number of keywords and phrases related to your book – these help your readers find your book when they are searching online for your topic or genre. Check how many you can input and use all of them, include both short phrases such as *folding napkins* and one or two long phrases such as *how to fold cloth napkins for a formal dinner party*.

If you have followed the methods for creating a title and writing a description you will already have a list of keywords and phrases. These methods included writing a list of all words and phrases related to your book and doing some online searches to see what else is suggested. There are online tools, e.g. Adwords, that can help you identify how many people are actually using your keywords and phrases; select those that are most commonly used, have little competition and are the best fit for your book.

Revisit this activity regularly and change your keywords and phrases as appropriate. Commonly used search terms change – there might be a sudden rush of people looking for beetroot recipes, if your book contains such a recipe then include this with your keywords. As some search engines use techniques to check that your keywords are not just a random selection of common search terms that have no relationship to your book it is worthwhile ensuring your keywords and phrases, or at least some of them, are included in your description.

Keywords and phrases play an integral role in getting your book onto the first page of search results; allocate time regularly to this activity, perhaps once a month, to ensure your book is seen by readers.

5 - Price

Your readers will take note of the price of your book and make a judgment about its quality and value, this judgment is the reader's perception rather than reality however it will influence their decision to buy.

The reader will have an expectation about what the price should be, much lower than this and they will perceive the book to be of poor quality, too high and the reader will believe the content does not provide value for money. You need to establish the right price based on the type of book you have written.

A specialist non-fiction book with a limited market may well command a high price tag, in fact it will be expected. Whereas a short novel promoted as a holiday read will probably require a lower price, however the market for holiday reads is bigger than for specialist non-fiction.

Getting the price right will also increase the number of buyers who actually read your book. A significant number of people buy books they never read, this is especially true of ebooks, particularly free downloads, but is also applies to printed books. Now you might think this doesn't matter as, after all, they have paid for the book and contributed to your income. However, if they don't read your book they won't write a review, they won't become a loyal fan, they won't buy your next book and they won't recommend your book to others. If they pay the right price for your book they will perceive it is of value to them, read it and recommend it.

There is, however, one advantage to pricing your book at a discounted price or making it available for free for a short period of time; sales and downloads will propel your book up the bestseller lists and increase its visibility. If you reduce the price for a fixed period, perhaps when you launch your book, ensure your readers know this is a special price for a limited time and inform them of the usual price; readers' perception of value will be based on the original price. This approach can also be used to develop a fan base for a series – the first book is discounted on a regular or permanent basis resulting in an increase in purchases, a number of these readers will then go on and purchase other titles in the series.

Maximising income
When deciding on the optimum price, or price range, for your book take into account the income you will achieve. Self-publishing services have a

range of royalty options dependent on your price and retail choices. If you publish an ebook using KDP you receive either 35% or 70% royalties depending on the book price (for some territories you also need to be enrolled onto KDP Select to receive 70%). If you price your book at £0.99/$0.99 you will receive 35%, sell 2000 books and you earn nearly £/$700. Price at £/$3.99 and you receive 70%, sell 1200 books and you earn nearly £/$840. Decide on your priority – sales, income, ranking, reviews, building a fan base – and price accordingly. A lower price does not always mean more sales, experiment until you have achieved the optimum price for your objectives.

Identifying the right price

There are a number of factors to take into account when pricing your book. These include minimum price to cover printing costs, price of other books similar to yours and perceived value of the book.

Take a look at the prices of other books similar to yours and in the categories you could place your book. Note the average price of the bestsellers – this is likely to be the highest price you can sell for.

Identify any minimum and maximum price you can charge based on your publication choices; if you publish using KDP you cannot offer your book elsewhere at a cheaper price. A printed book will have a minimum cost to cover printing and a margin for the publisher, anything above this is your profit. Your publisher/publishing service may have a pricing policy that indicates the allowable price range; also note any restrictions such as having a price that ends x.99.

Consider the length of your book, if you have written a short story or report then you will probably price at £0.99/$0.99, anything higher and you may not achieve sales because of perceived value. This may mean it is not cost effective to publish a printed version. If you write short stories or reports consider publishing a collection in order to achieve a higher price.

Charge the price of a cup of coffee! Some studies show that the optimum price for ebooks appears to be £2.99/$3.99, this is the price point that achieves maximum profit. This can be an excellent starting price for your ebooks whether fiction or non-fiction.

Price the different versions of your book separately. Generally a printed book is priced higher than an ebook, with an audio book being the most expensive. Ensure you link all versions of your book on your selected sales platform, you want your reader to be aware they can select an ebook or printed version and to take note of pricing differences – if an ebook is £/$3 cheaper than the printed version this will be perceived as good value.

Finally decide if you are going to price for individual currencies or base all prices on the USD price. I would recommend amending all prices so it appears the price has been given consideration, e.g. end with x.99 or x.49 rather than x.23. In some countries VAT is added to the price of ebooks, in Europe this is currently 3%. To ensure the price is displayed correctly you will need to calculate the pre VAT price; to sell at £/€2.99 you will need to price your book at £/€2.90.

Note: the retailer may change your price either because they price match or they have included your book in their own promotion – this may or may not effect your royalty payments.

Monitor the impact on both sales and income of different pricing strategies and review your objectives regularly. If appropriate change your price, either short term or long term, in order to achieve your goals.

6 - Publishing and Retail Options

If you self-publish you have considerable choice when deciding where to publish, how to publish and where to sell your book; some options are available for free whilst others have a cost attached.

Secure a traditional publishing contract and your publisher will have access to a wide range of retail outlets however, don't assume that your book will appear in all bookstores, in supermarkets or even on Amazon. Check your contract and with your publisher to find out where your book will appear. It is worthwhile negotiating with your publisher in order to gain maximum coverage for example making your book available as an ebook.

Self-publish and you have a wide range of options available to you. You could publish a printed book, ebook, audio book, or an enhanced ebook. Publish your ebook using KDP and your book will appear on Amazon; enrol onto KDP Select and you will you have access to some useful promotional tools however you will not be able to make your ebook available elsewhere. Publish your ebook using Smashwords and, subject to meeting their quality requirements, your book can be made available through iBookstore, KOBO, Barnes and Noble and WHSmith.

Publish using the CreateSpace's Print on Demand (POD) service and your book will be available on Amazon and, if you select them, other outlets including bookstores, libraries and academic institutions. You won't, however, be able to create a hardback version.

Use a self-publishing service and your book will be made available to a wide range of bookstores – both online and offline. Your book will be cheaper to produce than POD however you will need to pay up front for your print run and, should you find an error, you will not be able to make changes until you print another batch.

You can also choose to publish and sell your ebook through sites such as Clickbank which give you the opportunity to make use of affiliate marketing, or you could sell from your own website.

Create a printed version of your book and you can purchase copies to sell, or give away, at your talks, seminars or training events. You may also persuade the less obvious retailers to stock your book, perhaps on a sale or return basis. Consider your local store, a local bookshop, or tourist locations such as a museum or historic house. You could even set up your own stall at a small business fair.

It is vital to consider the preferences of your readers and ensure your book is readily available in their preferred format; children love the additional features – video and audio - enhanced ebooks offer, many readers like the convenience of ereaders and therefore prefer ebook format, some readers will search for a book online and then order it through their local bookstore, some readers are now choosing audio books that they can listen to in the car or whilst exercising.

The choices may seem endless and each has advantages and disadvantages. Decide what your priorities are, identify the needs of your readers, list the pros and cons for each option and make a decision that enables you to maximise promotional and sales opportunities. You can always add to your initial publishing and retail choices at a later stage or try different options as you discover more about your readers; for example you could initially publish an ebook using KDP and later publish through Smashwords. You might then decide to produce a printed version and even consider creating an audio book. Continuously review your options to ensure you are always making best use of the available opportunities.

7 - Getting Reviews

There are a number of factors that will take readers towards the checkout with your book in hand, one of these is reviews. These reviews might be on a book retailer's website such as Amazon, they could be on a book site such as Goodreads, they might be printed on the cover of your book, or they might be printed in newspapers and magazines. Readers check out reviews and consider any ratings, the more reviews you have with a high rating the more likely they are to buy.

So how do you go about getting reviews? There are a number of approaches you can take depending on where you want reviews to appear:

• Make your book available for free on Amazon or other sites and promote this. It is likely that a considerable number of books will be downloaded, however only a small number of readers will write you a review. Despite the low number this is an excellent way to build up your verified purchaser reviews.

• Send a copy of your book to a newspaper, magazine or radio station. This route can be challenging so give yourself the best possible chance of getting a review by making you or your book newsworthy – try a local newspaper or one that's local to the location in your book.

• Send your book to a professional reviewer – this may have a cost attached and it is important that you get an honest review.

• Ask other authors for reviews, this can be a reciprocal arrangement. As before ensure you ask for an honest review.

• Promote yourself and your book on Goodreads.com.

If terms and conditions allow save your reviews as you may be able to use them in future marketing material.

If you get a bad review don't fret, it is likely the reviewer does not agree with the concept of your book rather than your writing. Over time a poor rating will be averaged out. If the review is personal or particularly unsavoury you can ask the website owner to remove it. If you get a lot of poor reviews consider removing your book from sale and improving it; you could always republish as a new book and effectively start again.

8 - Engage with your Readers – Know your Readers

Imagine you have published a book and all of your readers want to buy and read it; all you have to do is tell them your book is available, reinforce the message that this is a book for them, and finally ensure there are no barriers to making that purchase; all a reader wants is a quick route to the checkout. Remember your readers want your book however, they won't come and find you – you have to find them.

Before you can develop a strategy to engage with your readers you need to know who they are and where they hang out. Many writers, when asked, will say that their readers are anyone and everyone; some writers will describe a large and diverse group such as parents; a small number of writers will have a clear idea, even a written description, of exactly who their readers are and where they can find them.

It is incredibly useful to define your target readers and divide them into groups, you can then describe one "typical" person from each group. The more you breakdown your groups into sub-groups and the more you know about each group the easier it will be to target your marketing activity and ensure you get a return on your investment of money or time.

Let's say you have written a cookery book and have defined a group of readers; most of this group have access to and use the internet and will regularly search for recipe ideas, a small number regularly use Facebook, most have an email account and access this every one or two days and they all enjoy watching cookery programs on TV.

Based on this small amount of information you can see immediately that setting up a Facebook page will bring limited returns from this particular group. You might decide to set up a food and cookery blog or website however your readers do not know about your site and, even with clever use of keywords, it will be a while before your readers discover you. Initially your time might be better spent identifying which websites your readers use and promote yourself and your book on these sites; offer to write a feature or guest blog or you could advertise on the site. Once you have developed a relationship with your readers direct them to your own website where you can further engage with them and capture their email addresses so that you can send out a regular email newsletter. Remember how your readers watch cookery programmes on TV, once you are communicating directly with them you could create a series of YouTube cookery videos and provide links to these from your website, blog or newsletter.

For some groups of readers the buyer may regularly be someone else, for example a parent, or the book may be purchased as a gift. Think about where the buyer hangs out with the reader or when in the role that defines them as the buyer; a parent might visit websites aimed at children or those aimed at parents. People who buy books as gifts are likely to browse bookstores, gift shops or check out a website of specific interest to the reader.

So how do you define your reader and discover where you can find them? Ask yourself, "*what type of person would benefit from or enjoy reading my book*?" Next complete a reader profile or profiles – an example of the type of questions you can ask is shown below. If you have multiple answers or a range for any of the characteristics or questions consider dividing them and creating sub-groups, for example if you have an age range of 24 – 65 consider dividing this into several age ranges; also consider dividing your group into male and female sub-groups, Ask yourself, *"would a 24 female read the same magazines as a 59 year old male?"* Of course your answer will depend on a lot of factors however if you were to write an article for a magazine aimed at women you can instantly see that you have not engaged with most men, if males are part of your target market you need to do something else as well. Remember you need to ask everyone in your target market to buy your book. You may end up with several reader profiles, this is great as you can really target your marketing activity.

Reader Profile

Age; Gender; Culture; Values; Goals; Priorities; Children/ages; Occupation; Income; Health; Hobbies; Sports; Interests; Car; Type of home; Education; Music; Problems faced; Radio stations; Newspapers; Magazines; Books; TV programmes; Politics; Preferred shops; Days out; Holidays; Meals out; Coffee shops; Gym; Clubs; Groups; Community activities; Any other information.

Once you have your reader profiles you can identify their hangouts. One way of doing this is to create a list of hangouts or activities you are happy to engage with – Facebook, email, High Street, local newspaper, magazines, websites - for each reader profile give the hangout a usage or visit rating of 0-5 with 0 being never and 5 being daily. You can now see where the majority of each group hangout and also any hangouts that are frequented by all reader groups. This information will really help you focus your energies.

Example list and ratings
Reader profile 1 – makes up 50% of total readers
Reader profile 2 – makes up 25% of total readers
Reader profile 3 – makes up 25% of total readers

Hangout – *Facebook*
Reader profile 1 visit/usage rating = 2
Reader profile 2 visit/usage rating = 2
Reader profile 3 visit/usage rating = 4

Hangout – *garden centres*
Reader profile 1 visit/usage rating = 3
Reader profile 2 visit/usage rating = 3
Reader profile 3 visit/usage rating = 3
Notes: possible talk or demonstration at garden centre for customers

Hangout – *named gardening magazine*
Reader profile 1 visit/usage rating = 4
Reader profile 2 visit/usage rating = 3
Reader profile 3 visit/usage rating = 1

Hangout – *named horticulture website*
Reader profile 1 visit/usage rating = 3
Reader profile 2 visit/usage rating = 5
Reader profile 3 visit/usage rating = 5
Notes: start own blog and offer to write content for website in exchange for link to blog

Hangout – *email*
Reader profile 1 visit/usage rating = 3
Reader profile 2 visit/usage rating = 5
Reader profile 3 visit/usage rating = 4
Notes: develop an email newsletter when email addresses captured

Hangout – *YouTube*
Reader profile 1 visit/usage rating = 2
Reader profile 2 visit/usage rating = 2
Reader profile 3 visit/usage rating = 4
Notes: start creating some video demonstrations

You now know where to focus your time however you can still undertake activities that appear to have limited appeal; you might enjoy them which is important, you might just want to see if you have any unidentified readers, or you may want to learn a new technique for future use. Over time review and add to this list as your knowledge and skills develop.

As you engage with your readers you build a relationship based on trust; always deliver on your promises and give them something worthwhile whether hints and tips or just make them laugh. As you develop this relationship your readers will become your fans – when this happens there will be a subtle shift in their behaviour, rather than you having to seek out your readers they will start looking for you. Your fans will actively search for you online, they will look out for and attend your public appearances, and they will seek out and buy your books. You will always need to engage new readers however your marketing activities will shift towards remaining connected with your fans.

9 - Engage with your Readers – Online

Many, possibly the majority, of your readers will engage online whether shopping, social media, viewing TV and videos or searching for information. These same readers are likely to turn to the internet if they have an offline engagement with you and want to find out more. Even if your readers rarely engage online you will need a minimum presence, possibly a website, in order to meet their expectations, some people do actually believe that if they can't find you online then you don't really exist!

There is a vast array of opportunities for you to engage with readers online however what you select depends on both your personal preference and that of your readers so do remember to check your reader profiles and ensure you go where they hangout. Once they have become your fans they will be happy to go where you hangout.

Website and blog
Creating a website and/or blog is easy to do and does not have to take too much time to set up and maintain. There are a number of providers that offer free and paid for services; if you are experienced or ready to invest time learning

about this area then you may want consider your needs and research the available services. If you want to get up and running quickly then consider services that require no experience, provide you with templates and make it easy for you to make changes and add content. Look at Moonfruit, Wordpress and Blogger, all offer free websites or blogs, all offer templates or themes, both Wordpress and Moonfruit offer additional paid for options. One advantage of Moonfruit is that they provide both the design tools for a wide range of website features combined with website hosting (some other services also provide this however others will only host your blog) so upgrading from a blog to a full blown website is straightforward.

Always check the terms and conditions of your provider as there may be some restrictions such as advertising or volume of traffic; some free sites will include their own adverts or branding.

You can create different elements of your blog or website on different sites and then use links so your readers can move smoothly between them; it is easy to set up a blog on Blogger and then have a page that links directly to another website with additional content. Taking this approach can be useful if you have built up a following on a blog only site and later decide to grow your site and offer additional features however, note that the templates and themes may be different.

Decide what to include on your site and how often you are going to update it. Think about what you need now and what you might need in the future. You don't have to do it all immediately however you may want to build up your site over time as you write new books and build a fan base. Below are a few things you might want to consider either now or in the future:

• Include a link to the sales page of your book – sounds obvious but you need to make it easy for your readers to buy. Having to search for your book is a barrier.

• Make use of keywords and phrases - you should have plenty from the exercises to create a title and write a description - this will help readers find you on the internet. Use these phrases in your website description, metadata (look at the design tools or admin section of your site), blog posts and articles. Never force keywords into your writing however include them wherever possible.

• Update your site at least once a week; in the early days you might even want to consider updating every two or three days. Search engines tend to give a higher ranking to sites that are updated regularly with quality content.

• Have a question and answer section – if you do ensure you respond to readers' queries.

• Promote your new book before it is published, this can help create anticipation; you could provide snippets or even the first chapter on your site.

• Have a contacts page – if you want readers to contact you. Have an email address that you use specifically for fan mail or mail related to your book; check it regularly and respond.

• Make use of any available analysis or monitoring tools; these can be useful if you want to know when readers visit your site.

• Capture email addresses so you can offer your readers a regular newsletter or inform them of special offers.

• Offer free stuff – an ebook, audio file or sample chapter.

- Include a gallery - include images relating to you and your book. These could include locations, your launch party, and any personal appearances.

- Write your own interview – you can ask yourself some questions and answer them. Look at other interviews for inspiration, think about what you would like to ask another author or any other person. These questions can relate to writing, values, most admired person, favourite holiday destination, plans for future books, or advice for writers or those interested in the topic of your book.

Domain name
Whenever you set up a website or blog you will be asked to create a domain name, your initial domain name will automatically include the name of the service provider. In order to use your own domain name you will need to purchase this and then assign it to your site; some providers enable you to do this directly from within their admin section. When selecting a name, or names, ensure you choose one that clearly reflects the content and purpose of your site – this might be your brand, name, penname, book title, series title or the subject of your book. It might take several attempts to find a name that is available.

Also decide if you want your site name to end .co.uk, .com or any of the others that are available; you can of course decide to buy several. Note that you purchase domain names for a fixed period of time, usually two years, so you will need to renew it if you wish to keep that name.

Facebook
If you have a Facebook account then you can create Facebook pages to engage with your target readers – your page does not have to have a direct link to your personal Facebook details and posts so you can choose to keep these only available to family and friends whilst your Facebook page is available to your readers. You can name the page with your book title, series title, character name or author name. You can sign your posts with any name you choose – this is great if you use a pen name.

Once you have created your page you can direct readers to it or you can use Facebook tools to advertise your page to targeted groups; there is a cost however you set your budget. Post on your page regularly, in the early stages once or twice a day is good. You can use this page to promote your books, events and personal appearances;

you could even promote specific blog posts or content on your website.

This is an excellent way of engaging with readers who are regular users of Facebook as, once they have liked your page your posts may appear on their Newsfeed giving a constant reminder about and update on your books.

Email newsletter
If you have captured email addresses you can send regular newsletters to your readers. This newsletter should be of worth to the reader so think carefully about the content. You might write an article related to the subject of your book, you could create a mini ecourse and send out a new section each week or you could inform your readers of any book promotions you are running. There are many email capture and management tools available that can be used on your website or other web presence – one example is AWeber.

YouTube
YouTube enables you to upload and share your videos with others. Initially you may think that creating a video is not for you however, think again, video is for everybody and, considering the number of people using YouTube, it is likely you can find some of your readers here.

If you are not yet familiar with YouTube then go to the website and do a search on any topic, perhaps something you want to know how to do. Whatever it is you will find several videos, there are lots of funny, how to, academic, learning, promotional and other types of videos.

You can create a video using moving images, a series of still images, text, voice and music. You could even create an animation. If you have yet to develop your skills in this area then start by creating a presentation style video – using presentation software – with a series of slides containing images and text and then add music or voiceover. Save the presentation as a video and upload.

There are lots of possibilities for your video - you could give a reading from your book, create a book trailer, give a talk or demonstration on a topic in your book, develop a video course, create a tourist information video of the locations in your book, get someone to interview you, or create a video blog.

You can share the link to your video on your Facebook page, in your newsletter, on your website and in your books.

As an alternative to YouTube take a look at Vimeo; you could post your videos on both platforms.

Guest blog

If your readers hangout at a particular blog or website then ask if you can write a guest blog or article. Initially you might just end the blog with your name or pen name, later, as you get a good reputation, you can add a link to your website or other online content. Always be professional when guest blogging, write quality content and ensure you check the blog regularly for comments and respond to these where appropriate.

Online article writing

There are many sites that allow you to submit and publish articles on a wide variety of subjects. Your articles can be accompanied by an info box which contains details of your book and links to your website. Have a look at ezinearticles.com it is easy to set up an account and start submitting articles, you can also write using multiple pen names. As with guest blogging ensure you write quality content, readers will make a judgment about the quality of your books based on your articles.

Twitter

Twitter is a social networking service that enables people to tweet text messages up to 140 characters in length. Set up an account and build a following, follow others, retweet messages and respond to tweets. This is one area where it is preferable not to directly advertise your book or ask people to buy it. However you could tweet about what you are doing, comment on a news item or say how you feel about today's book launch. Another way to use Twitter is to write a short story, poem or feature within the maximum character count. If you can provide something entertaining or useful then your followers may retweet your tweet and you can reach a huge number of people. If people are engaged, helped, or entertained then they will find out more about you and what you have to offer.

Webinars

Have you considered running a webinar – or a web based seminar? These provide massive opportunities to engage with your readers. If you have written a non-fiction book then why not run a webinar on this subject. For a fiction book you might discuss the process of developing your characters or locations. Create a presentation prior to the event and include video, audio, links to websites in fact anything you can show on screen or hear through audio.

You can choose how much interaction your audience has – typically the audience will type in messages and questions which you can then answer live or save until later and provide a FAQ page on your website or through email. You can also record the webinar so that you can make it available after the event. You could run a webinar to a small, perhaps personally selected, group and then make the recording available after the event.

If you are inviting comment and questions during the event you might like to have an assistant who can group the questions together or draw your attention to those that you could answer live during your session.

Consider offering attendees something special as a thank-you for attending, you could include a download link to free content such as an ebook that is available for 24 hours only.

There is a wide range of online webinar providers available including free, free trial, and paid for services; some free and trial versions will have restrictions. Take your time to find a service that meets your needs. You need reliability so check recommendations, the ability to accommodate your chosen audience size, and the ability to record – I would recommend this function as you then have the files for later use.

First time around can be nerve wracking especially if you haven't given a presentation before or don't feel comfortable with technology – try attending an online webinar first so you get a feel for how they work.

Online radio show
Did you know you can broadcast your own online radio show? There are a number of online radio services and apps you can download to record and broadcast your show. Have a look at blogradiotalk.com and spreaker.com to see what is possible. You could interview guests, give a talk about your book or have a discussion about the topic of your book. The show does not have to be related to your book, you could be promoting yourself. There are free and paid for options available so you can give it a try without any outlay and later, as your fan base grows, pay for additional features as you want them.

Author pages

Many online publisher and book retailers provide an author page for you to provide an author bio and information about or links to your books; some enable you to create different author pages for your separate pen names all within the same account.

Write your bio in the third person and include any information that is relevant or interesting – both personal and professional. For example – *Jane Smith has worked for many years as a chef in one of London's top restaurants. She has developed and perfected many recipes and has made these available in her books. Having recently travelled to Africa and experienced both the culture and traditional cooking techniques…. She now runs her own restaurant in the centre of Bath….*

Update your bio as you publish new books or have new experiences that are worth sharing with your readers.

Goodreads

The Goodreads author program provides you with opportunities to promote yourself and your books to readers. With over 20 million members you are sure to find some that are looking for a book like yours.

You can create an author bio, write a blog and publicise your events. You can also add a widget to your website so that visitors can read reviews of your book.

Hold an online launch party
Create anticipation for and interest in your book by publicising a launch date and inviting all of your readers to the party.

You can create your online event using a Facebook page, webinar, blog or radio show. Whichever you choose ensure you have the facility for partygoers to engage with you and each other.

Plan the event and provide a timetable of activities. You might start the event by thanking people for attending and then giving a short introduction to yourself and your new book. During the event you could give a reading from the book, hold a question and answer session, have an online quiz or game, giveaway freebies such as the first chapter of your book and hold a competition with a copy of your book as the prize.

You could prepare some of the activities in advance – for example a video of yourself discussing your book, a short quiz or a website with digital freebies to download during the event. Ensure that you create a link to your book's sales page to make it easy for partygoers to buy your book at the event.

You might make your book available at a reduced price for the duration of the event telling your partygoers that they are the only people who will be told about this discounted price.

At the end of the event thank people for attending and provide a follow up gift to those who provide their email address.

Audio
Create an audio file that readers can listen to whilst driving, walking or exercising. You could record a seminar on a topic related to your book, an interview with yourself or anyone else, a training session, some practical hints and tips, an interview with someone who has successfully used the content of your book, a short story or even make your entire book available as an audio book.

Once created make your file available on your website, you might decide to give it away as a gift or to sell it. You could create a series of audio files or podcasts that together form an entire course related to the subject of your book.

All you need is basic digital recording equipment, this could be a microphone connected to your computer or a smartphone. Once you have recorded your audio file save it as mp3 or other suitable format and then upload the file to your website.

Online advertising
Direct advertising generally has a cost attached so it is important to set a budget and consider the returns you expect. There are several options for online advertising, consider your readers and decide where your money and efforts are best spent.

Google Adwords
You can create a text advert that provides a link to your book's sales page or your website; this is displayed to internet users when they search for selected keywords or visit specific sites. A tool is available to help you select the keywords and phrases based on the number of people using

those search terms and the competition from other advertisers.

Monitor the cost of click throughs and the conversion rate from clicks to sales. If each click cost you £0.30 and you have a conversion rate of 10% they each sale will cost you £3.00. However if each click costs you £0.10 and you have a conversion rate of 25% then each book sale costs you £0.40.

Goodreads

This book site has an advertising program that allows you to advertise your book to a targeted selection of their 20 million members. You pay in advance and each time your advert is clicked your account is debited.

Online book clubs and book lists

There are a large number of other online book clubs and book lists that offer paid for and free advertising opportunities. Your book is listed on the website and, in some cases, included in an email list sent to members.

If you are making your book available for free some websites provide opportunities to advertise your book at no cost during the period it is free.

These include pixelofink.com and addictedtoebooks.com.

In app advertising

If you use a smartphone you have probably noticed that some apps carry adverts – often these are the free apps. As many people use free apps you could give this a go; your advert can include a link through to your website or book's sales page. There are a wide range of options and costs available from text based adverts through to full blown video with interactive features.

Facebook

You can create an advert on Facebook with a link through to either a Facebook page or website. You set a daily budget and the dates you want your advert to show, you also select who to show it to – gender, age range, location, interests – so that your ad is targeted giving you a better return. Ensure you know what you want the readers who click through to your page or site to do, ultimately you want them to buy your book however you might decide to collect their email address in return for free stuff and then promote your book through an email newsletter.

Other websites

If you know of a website that is frequented by large numbers of your readers then consider placing an advert on that site. Think about what kind of advert you would like and where it needs to be positioned then approach the website owners - there is often a contact number or email address available. If you have a limited budget consider what you can offer in exchange for advertising space – perhaps some content for their site.

Search Engine Optimisation (SEO)

If you have any kind of web presence then sooner or later you will come across the term SEO; this is essentially ensuring your website or other web presence is visible and appears on the first pages of search results. You can pay specialists to "optimise" your site, however be aware this is an ongoing job as search engines such as Google regularly change the way they rank sites and they don't share this information. Using a specialist service may not provide any return on investment for a writer however there are some simple things you can do; you don't have to do all of these right away, just allocate a little time each week or month to undertaking one or two tasks.

Identify keywords and phrases

Use the results from the activities you completed when creating a title, in particular those used to identify common search terms related to the subject or genre of your book. There are some useful tools to help with this including Google's Adword tool. This list of keywords and phrases can then be used for the SEO activities below. Remember to check and update these regularly as frequently used search terms change.

Description

Look in the admin section of your website or blog and you will likely find a description box. Complete this using a style that will attract click-through as this may be shown in search results. In order to write the description make some notes on what your site is about, who it is aimed at, the benefits it offers and, most importantly, what people might enter into a search engine when looking for your type of site.

Keywords

It is likely that within the admin and specific content sections, (blog posts, pages), of your website you have the option to add keywords and phrases; make best use of these. Again research commonly used search terms and phrases related to your site and the content on your site.

Links from other sites

There has been quite a lot said about whether this still has value – this works two ways, either readers are viewing the other site and then click through to your site or internet search engine spiders follow these links and catalogue them. As we speak sites that contain only lots of links to other sites are likely to be of little value, links from sites that are already have a high ranking are likely to be more worthwhile. It can be worthwhile writing guest blogs or submitting to quality online article sites and including a link to your blog/website.

Update content

The easiest way to do this is to have a blog and post at least once a week. If you prefer you can write regular articles, hints and tips, or other updates to your website. Where possible include some keywords and phrases in these posts or content, though don't force it, the content must be of use or entertaining to the reader.

There are a lot of opportunities to engage with your readers online, consider where your readers hangout, engage with them and start building a relationship. Develop your skills and experience of different online platforms and make use of them to meet with even more readers. Build your own web presence and, as your readers become fans, they will come to you. And remember — have fun!

10 - Engage with your Readers – Offline

There are massive opportunities to engage with your readers offline, in this age of social media it can be easy to forget that you don't always need a computer, tablet or Smartphone to find, meet and engage with your readers.

There are considerable benefits to undertaking at least some of your marketing activity offline including being able to engage with readers who do not use social media on a regular basis and, if the engagement is face-to-face, you get immediate feedback on the effectiveness of the activity.

Consider the activities below and decide where you are most likely to find your readers and which you will most enjoy. If you feel a little nervous about appearing on TV or running a workshop then start with some of the other activities that enable you to develop your skills and confidence, you might even decide to take a course on teaching and training or public speaking.

Newspapers
Write an article or feature for a community, local or national newspaper; this could be a paid for article or you could write it for free. Local papers

in particular are regularly looking for fillers so if you are ready with a piece that enables you to promote yourself or your book whilst writing about or reporting on something of local interest then you could end up with considerable column inches; provide photos and your chances of getting into print go up considerably. Even if you are providing material for free remember that this is no more work and considerably less expensive than creating an advert and, because the piece has local interest, it is more likely to be read.

As an author you are of local interest and newsworthy, you could ask a reporter to interview you or provide an interview ready for printing. People are always interested in people so ask yourself what would interest other people about you and your life – this might be an unusual job, how you overcame adversity, perhaps a challenge you undertook, or maybe how you became a writer.

Approach a newspaper and offer to write a regular feature on a specific topic or a general opinion piece. If writing for a community paper then you could offer to do this for free. As your purpose is to ultimately promote your book then consider how this will happen – maybe end the piece with your name and author of... or perhaps your website, blog or Twitter address. You could get known as the expert in your field – this will definitely boost your book sales.

Create a press release for any significant events, for example the launch of your new book, a challenge you are undertaking (running a marathon) or you opening the school fete. You could follow this up with an after the event feature or report.

Magazines
Write a short story, submit a feature, send in a letter – again you are looking to promote your name as a writer and, where possible, your book. Some magazines provide a short intro to their writers at the beginning of the magazine.

Enter magazine writing competitions – these can be great for raising your profile because the name and a bio of the winner, and sometimes the runners up, is printed.

Have you considered doing a real life feature? Not only will you raise your profile but you will also get paid. If this is where your readers hangout then this really is a worthwhile investment of your time. Read a few features to see what sort of stories are printed – often these are overcoming adversity - think about your life and identify some of the challenges you have faced. Obviously only write about those you are happy to share.

Radio
Approach your local radio station and ask them to interview you or invite you as a guest on a show. This could be a general chat about your book, your life or your opinions on topical subjects. You could however also offer to do a question and answer session on a subject related to your book, listeners ring in and, live on air, ask how to prune roses, save money booking a holiday or any other subject you have written about.

TV
There are opportunities for writers to be interviewed on TV. Local news channels are always on the lookout for people stories and are particularly interested in your back story – perhaps you lost your job and started writing to make some extra money or maybe you nearly gave up and decided to give it one last try. Whatever your story viewers are interested in you.

Guest speaker

Be a guest speaker at any event or group meeting attended by your readers. This can be a great opportunity to promote and sell your book. You could speak about any subject whether related to your book or not. You might talk about working from home, achieving your goals or on the topic of your book.

Seminar/training/workshop event

Running a seminar is an ideal way to promote yourself and your book. You have a captive audience and, if they enjoy your session, they will buy your book; ensure you have copies with you if available in printed form or provide information on where it can be purchased.

You could run your own seminar or offer to do one for an organisation. This could be on any subject you like; if you have written a non-fiction book then you could base the seminar on this topic and establish yourself as an expert. If you have written a fiction book then you could run a session on writing, motivation, time management, planning – or anything else that you have experience of.

Use the opportunity to raise your profile by providing a delegate pack with useful freebies.

The type of products you want in your pack are things that people will keep and use. Consider a travel mug, a desk clock or an item related to your topic; if you are discussing time management then you could include a branded desk planner. If you have written a series of books why not consider providing one book in your delegate pack. These items have a cost however you can charge entry for your own event or a fee if you are speaking for an organisation.

Book reading
You could do a book reading at a library, bookstore, school, youth club, interest groups, book club or almost anywhere. Select the extract with care so that that it engages your audience and encourages them to want more. Practise reading your extract to ensure you are familiar with it, I know you wrote it but is surprising how easy it is to forget what comes next. End on a cliffhanger however leave the audience satisfied.

Book signing
If your book is available in your local bookstore – or any other retail outlet – then do a book signing. Be sure to promote the event well to generate interest. If your bookstore does not yet stock your book ask them if they will – many national bookshops can make local decisions. Some

bookshops and retailers will happily rent you a table for the day for either a fee or commission on sales.

Rent a table at an event

If your readers attend craft events, table top sales, or gift fairs then why not rent a table and sell your book. Be available to answer questions, provide advice related to writing or your book's topic or just to chat. If appropriate you could even have an activity area where readers can try out your ideas. Remember people come to these events to buy.

Attend networking events

Attend a networking event relevant to you and one your readers might attend, this could be a local small business breakfast club. Not only will you have the opportunity to promote yourself you may also be offered other opportunities, perhaps to run a training session, and meet people with skills you could utilise. Don't openly give out a leaflet promoting your book, make the connections first and then swap business cards.

Open an event/be a judge

As a published writer you are a local celebrity; you might not think that now but do your promotional work and you soon will be. Offer to open your local fete or charity event, or be a judge at the local baking competition or carnival. Make the most of the opportunity without overpowering the main event; be available to chat with your readers, provide a copy of your book for the raffle, and have business cards handy to give out when people ask for your details.

Offline advertising
Magazines and newspapers
You can advertise your book in a specialist or general magazine targeted at your readers. This can be expensive so you may need to think of this as a long term investment. When creating this type of advert ensure you include details on how to buy your book.

The greater the distribution and the more affluent the readership of the magazine, the more expensive your advert is likely to be. Try local magazines and newspapers if their distribution reaches your target readers. One way to reduce the cost is to write an advertorial which, as well as advertising your book, includes useful information or advice; a newspaper or magazine may offer you a reduced rate or extra space at no additional cost.

Radio and TV

Local radio and TV may offer some reasonably priced advertising packages; consider your readers and when they might be watching or listening, also think about the length and content of your adverts. Whilst prime time adverts may not bring any return on your investment there could be some benefit with the off peak deals.

Other books

You can advertise your book within other books. If you have written other books then it is straightforward to advertise "other books by this author," you can also contact other self-published authors and ask if they would like to advertise your book in exchange for you advertising theirs.

Launch party

Have a book launch party, hire a venue, invite friends, colleagues and the press, put on some nibbles and drinks and send your book out there in the style it deserves. Start the party by introducing yourself and your book, thank any contributors and supporters, and give a book reading.

Prepare promotional packs for your guests and press packs for journalists. Have copies of your book available to purchase and give away copies in a raffle.

You could link this to your online launch and provide opportunities for your online guest to join in the fun.

Take photographs, or ask others to take them for you, and record any speeches you give. You can then use these with other promotional activities such as your blog or a magazine feature.

Whilst having a launch party is all about promoting your book, as with all your activities, ensure you enjoy it and have fun.

Make good use of offline promotional activities as they give your readers the chance to really get to know you and also provide you with the opportunity to find out more about your readers. When readers want to meet you face to face they have become real fans.

11 - Develop a Marketing Plan

Creating a marketing strategy or plan can be as simple as a sheet of paper with information about your readers, how you are going to engage with them, which activities you are going to prioritise, and how much time you are going to devote to marketing and promotion. As you promote your book you will review, adapt and further develop this plan.

It is important to consider your budget as you develop your marketing plan; initially you might have a zero or small budget, that's not a problem as there is a lot you can do for no cost. As you start to make sales it is worth allocating some of your profit to marketing and promotion however, it is important to spend your budget on those activities that will bring you the greatest returns or help you to achieve your goals – you might have the budget for a prime time TV advert however that budget could be better spent on commissioning a new cover or placing an advert on a carefully selected website.

If you have worked through the previous chapters you will have a clear idea about who your readers are and which marketing activities will help you engage with them. You are now at the stage of prioritising, planning, doing and reviewing.

Below is an example of how you might develop and present your plan; it is a working document that you will add to and amend as you review the effectiveness of your activities, develop your own skills and new opportunities become available.

Marketing and promotion plan
Planned activity - current
1) Set up a website
Purpose: to have a web presence that enables readers to find me as the author and also to promote my books. As people engage with the site additional features will be added.

Deadline: 10th April

Budget: £0

Tasks

1) Consider and plan requirements
 - Time required – 2 hours
 - Deadline - 25th March
2) Research and select a provider
 - Time required – 1 hour
 - Deadline - 27th March
3) Set up basic pages using templates
 - Time required – 4 hours
 - Deadline – 2nd April

4) Purchase and assign a domain name
 - Time required – 30 minutes
  - Deadline - 3rd April
5) Write and upload some web content
 - Time required – 8 hours
 - Deadline – 8th April
6) Website goes live – 8th April
7) Update content
 - Time required - 2 hours a week initially, reduce down to 30 minutes a week once there is sufficient content
Review date: 31st June
Notes: At a later stage add an email capture feature.

2) Offer and promote book as free for a limited period

Purpose: to get downloads in order to improve sales ranking and get reviews.
Deadline: 30th March
Tasks
1) Set dates when book is available for free
 - Time required – 15 minutes
 - Deadline – 24th March
2) Promote book as free on various book websites
 - Time required – 1 hour

- Deadline various – based on the requirements of the book website, some require listing on first day book is free (write in dates here)
3) Monitor downloads and sales ranking
- Time required – 10 minutes daily during free period
Review date: 28th April and 28th May – this allows enough time for reviews to be written and impact on sales to be monitored
Notes: Monitor sales at usual price following this free period.

3) Give a book reading
Purpose: to meet with readers and create a worthwhile experience that will result in them wanting to read the book.
Deadline: 15th July
Tasks
1) Contact local libraries offering to read to children
- Time required – 3 hours in total
- Deadline – 4th June
2) Book in dates
- Time required – 1 hour
- Deadline – 12th June
3) Select and practise reading extract
- Time required – 4 * 1 hour sessions
- Deadline – base on date of first reading
Review date: 18th August

Notes: Plan both weekday and weekend readings where possible.

Planned activity - near future
Set up blog
Create a press pack
Create a mini course to offer as a free download on website

Regular activities – ongoing
Update Facebook page – daily
 - Time required – 15 minutes
Update website – weekly
 - Time required – 30 minutes

Regular activities - occasional
Book signing
Write a newspaper article
Update press pack

Supporting tasks and actions
Research and record information about local independent bookstores
Investigate available marketing items for guest/delegate packs – pens, mugs

Personal development to support marketing and promotion

Learn to create a video from presentation slides and with voiceover

Undertake some training on delivering a talk to a group

Future marketing activities, tasks and ideas

Create a series of videos and upload to YouTube or Vimeo

Capture email addresses on website

Review publishing options

Publish book as a paperback and promote

Enrol onto KDP Select and plan use of promotional tools

Commission a new book cover when budget allows

Write articles for online magazines

Organise an interview with local newspaper

A plan similar to the one above is all you need to organise your marketing activities and start promoting your book. If you prefer you can present your plan in a table or use specialist software. Whichever you choose ensure you prioritise your activities and allocate sufficient time to completing them.

Create a brand

As you develop your plan it is worth thinking about your brand. The brand could be you as the author, a book character or a book series. As a writer you may well have multiple brands to suit different aspects of your writing business.

You could decide to let your brand evolve naturally, readers will refer to you and your work depending on what they notice, perhaps, "there's always a pair of pink shoes in her books," which will evolve into the Pink Shoes brand.

Once you have created your brand or brands ensure you link all associated books, websites, press packs and public events to that brand. Create a logo, which can be as simple as the brand name in a selected font type and colour, and use it on all of your marketing material.

You can create a brand now and, if you find it's not working for you or is sending the wrong message, change it later.

Time management

Marketing, promotion and selling your book can take up considerable time, in fact you may find yourself so caught up in these activities that you have little or no time left for writing. As you set up campaigns, write guest blogs and reply to posts on Facebook it is easy for the end of the day to come and your next book is no further forward. It is important to allocate enough time to promotion however this has to be in proportion to your goals. Prior to and immediately following publication you will need to dedicate a considerable percentage of your writing time to promotion; there might be a number of weeks when you spend 100% of your time on these activities.

One way to approach this is to plan your time based on your priorities. Use a diary or other planning tool, decide how much time you are going to allocate to promoting your book, identify which activities you are going to do and when – perhaps 15 minutes every day on Facebook and one blog post a week. You might also allocate 30 – 60 minutes a week to researching new opportunities and/or learning how to use new tools.

Ensure you allocate some time to monitoring the impact of your activities - sales, reviews, likes on Facebook – in some cases online tools help with this however you may have to make a best guess. Monitoring will help you decide where to focus your energies.

Try and plan in at least a small amount of writing time every day, this can be a journal entry at the end of the day however, remember that writing blog posts and articles do count as writing. Two or three weeks after the launch of your book plan your next project and allocate sufficient time to completing it; once you have completed your next book your priorities will likely shift back to marketing, promotion and selling.

12 - What Next?

You've written, published and have started to promote your book, your sales are growing and you are actively engaging with your readers. What should you do next?

1) Continue to develop and maintain the relationship you have with your readers, it is important to keep them with you and provide them with interesting and useful snippets; if you lose them now it will be harder to get them back later:

- If you have a Facebook page post regularly
- Update your webpage and post blogs at least once a week
- Send a newsletter regularly, once a fortnight is fine
- Run or speak at events.

2) Write your next book:

- Write your next book as soon as possible, you have fans waiting for it.

3) Review and amend your book:

- Is the cover attracting readers?
- Do you have any errors?

- Do you have a killer title?
- Are reviews highlighting any shortcomings?

4) Identify new ways to promote your book:

- Engage with blogs, newsletters or writing magazines to ensure you are aware of new opportunities
- Use Facebook advertising
- Give a talk or book reading.

And finally!

Start promoting your book today, even if you haven't written it yet. You can start a blog or Facebook page and discuss your subject or start building interest in your characters. If you have written some of your book why not upload the first chapter to a book site or your web page and receive some feedback. If you have published your book use some of the available promotional tools such as Amazon Countdown Deals to get your book seen and bought.

Wherever you are in your writing journey it is never too early to start promoting your book.

If you would like further hints and tips on writing then go to the Write it!:

blog at www.writepublishsell.blogspot.co.uk/

Or

Facebook page at
www.facebook.com/writepublishsell

Other Books by Adam Jackson

Write it!
How to write your book in 30 hours or less

Adam Jackson

Whether you are a published writer or just starting out on your writing journey Write it! will provide you with an approach that supports you getting your writing done.

The digital revolution has changed the publishing scene for writers and readers alike. No longer is the reader restricted to those books a publisher deems fit for the market. Writers can now reach markets that were previously closed to them opening up a whole host of opportunities to become a part-time or full-time writer earning an income that reflects their efforts.

If you are ready to start working towards becoming a published writer then Write It! is the perfect guide to writing your book fast. In just 30 hours you could have your work ready for publication. Depending on how much time you commit to writing you could become a published writer in just one week from now.

You will be able to:

- Identify your time thieves and create the time to write.

- Set up an effective office with the minimum of equipment.

- Generate an endless list of ideas; in fact you will never be without an idea again.

- Plan your book using a method that best suits your way of working.

- Write fast. Never again be sat at a computer wondering what to write next.

- Edit your work to ensure readers not only want to read your book but will come back time and time again for more.

This method can be used each and every time you write a book, or any other piece of written work, enabling you to start working from home and building up your writing business.

Publish it!

How to self-publish your book for free using Kindle Direct Publishing (KDP), CreateSpace and Smashwords

Adam Jackson

Self-publishing offers incredible opportunities for all writers regardless of the genre, subject or word count. You can write and publish short stories, poems, reports, novels; in fact whatever type of book you have written you can make it available to readers who are actively seeking new and exciting fiction and non-fiction books. The traditional gatekeepers of published works can no longer restrict what is available to the reader.

The benefits of self-publishing are so great that this option is now the first choice for many writers. As the writer and publisher you keep control of price, distribution, cover design, promotion and updates.

Using online services you can publish a printed or ebook for free and have it available to readers in as little as 10 minutes.

Follow the step-by-step instructions in this book and you will be able to:

- Select the best publishing option for you and your book.
- Prepare your book for publication.
- Publish your book for free.
- Select your distribution channels.
- Sell on Amazon, iBookstore, WHSmith, Barnes and Noble, and through other retailers.
- Start selling you book in as little as 10 minutes.
- Keep the profits from your book - royalties can be as high as 85%.
- Maximise sales and income using an effective pricing strategy.
- Write a description to ensure readers find your book online.

There is a huge demand for books by previously unpublished writers; tap into this market and develop a following of readers who will come back time after time to purchase and read your latest work.

This is one market where you are not in direct competition with other writers; if readers enjoy books written on a particular subject or in a specific genre they will look for, and buy, more of the same.

Daily Writing Prompts
30 prompts to get you writing every day

Adam Jackson

Write every day and you will achieve your writing goals. This book will help you develop a daily writing habit. It contains 30 writing prompts (it takes 30 days to form a new habit) and space for you to free write in order to warm up your writing muscles, ignite your creativity and ensure you ward off any signs of writers block.

Once you have warmed up those writing muscles and unleashed your creativity you can easily tackle those bigger writing goals.

Use the writing prompts again and again. You may even decide to develop some of your scribblings into a complete piece.